KEITH WALDROP

Transcendental Studies

A Trilogy

D1216210

GAULOISES

C A P O R A L

20 CIGARETTES

JACNO

GAULOISES®

RÉGIE FRANÇAISE DES TABACS
PHILIP MORRIS INC., RICHMOND, VA.
20 CLASS A CIGARETTES
MADE IN U.S.A.

Transcendental Studies

NEW CALIFORNIA POETRY

edited by	Robert Hass
	Calvin Bedient
	Brenda Hillman
	Forrest Gander

KEITH WALDROP

Transcendental Studies

A Trilogy

 University of California Press   Berkeley Los Angeles London

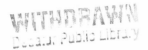

The publisher gratefully acknowledges the generous
contribution to this book provided by Judith Taylor.

University of California Press, one of the most distinguished
university presses in the United States, enriches lives around
the world by advancing scholarship in the humanities, social
sciences, and natural sciences. Its activities are supported by
the UC Press Foundation and by philanthropic contributions
from individuals and institutions. For more information,
visit www.ucpress.edu.

University of California Press
Berkeley and Los Angeles, California

University of California Press, Ltd.
London, England

Library of Congress Cataloging-in-Publication Data

Waldrop, Keith.
    Transcendental studies : a trilogy / Keith Waldrop.
        p.   cm. — (New California poetry ; 27)
    ISBN 978-0-520-25877-8 (cloth : alk. paper)
    ISBN 978-0-520-25878-5 (pbk. : alk. paper)
    I. Title.

PS3573.A423T73   2009
811'.54—dc22   2008025928

Manufactured in the United States of America

18   17   16   15   14   13   12   11   10   09
10   9   8   7   6   5   4   3   2

The paper used in this publication meets the minimum require-
ments of ANSI/NISO Z39.48–1992 (R 1997) (Permanence of Paper).

Contents

Shipwreck in Haven

I can't swim at all, and it is dangerous to converse with an unaccustomed Element.

ERASMUS

for Michael Gizzi

ONE

I

Balancing. Austere. Life-
less. I have tried to keep
context from claiming you.

Without doors. And there are
windows. How far, how
far into the desert have we come?

Rude instruments, product
of my garden. Might also be
different, what I am thinking of.

So you see: it is
not symmetrical, dark
red out of the snow.

2

Enemies for therapy, the
rind of the lime tree
in elaborate garlands.

Strew the table. Let the hall
be garlanded and lit, the will
to break away. Welcome your couches.

Witness these details. Your judgment, my
inclination. Hear. Touch. Taste.
Translate. Fixed: the river.

Disquieting thought, I am not
ultimate, full moon, memory.
Prepare for rout.

3

Here, even, in the
sand. Among the rocks, I have
heard, remnant of a cloud.

Unfleshed, short, thin, pointed.
Independent of you, a
revelation. A great city.

Flatly unknown, you do not
know of yourself, do not know
yourself, not stuck full of nails.

Under such illumination, darkness
becomes terror. Under this high
wall, dark ground.

4

High marble wall, broken mid-
way. Dark unphenomenality, like
the hand of a clock. Sun baked.

No *direct* communication likely. Marble
terrace. Suffusing with soft-
tinted glow. Images first.

The gods and you come later, a wealth
of approaches. Within the portico:
marble. Bundled like qualities.

Not—the world—one of
several, as if it could be
different. Nothing. Nothing different.

5

I mean translated, though some
charms are predetermined. Shall I
not delve and deliver?

If I could think it. Our
wings are broken. As easily might
plunge. In a violent sweat.

The desert. And might be
the same: lemurs
swim down gutters.

And might be threshold, never
hesitate, ship on the high sea.
The desert in the house.

6

Intrinsic, your un-
thinkability. Casts over all created
things annihilating shadow.

An opening for possible
storms, as a deity enters
the world, a stranger.

The bed we are not in: can-
not surprise it. What passes
in the street? Pure picture.

In the world these
limits, almost occult—only signals
corporeal. To think of something.

7

I was hardly dead, when you
called. Now are you convinced?
Infinitely soft strum.

As if night. As if im-
perceptibly. Slowly you fall. Break
somewhat the blackness of the day.

Might also be any
direction, every start
takes us to other time.

Forth across the sands. From
sky or from the liver,
divined. Endless beginning.

8

Need not end. Indeed, *nothing.* Step
out. Grist for wits. Shadow of your
shell. Stand there.

No other ground. No
other. And the world concerns you every-
where, but do not identify with it.

Let light onto us. Flowers through the
gate, flowers skimming
the wall. A carpet of petal.

Treasures below the earth. Neither in
this world nor another, guarding.
Nothing but fade and flourish.

9

Now there is a door and whoever
very beautiful and very
very strange. Near you a table.

Laughing. Singing. Calling to one
another, the crack of whips. Cloud to
cloud in ricochet.

Music of hooves and wheels. The heavenly
Jerusalem from shards of Babylon
destroyed. Now a door.

Where thinking ends, house and temple
echo, possible objects of
admiration. Will you go?

10

Oh yes and wheels on the pavement,
angels of incidence, rebounding from
waves, but precisely. Reflective angels.

Like the hand of a clock which, minute
by minute, crosses its appointed
spaces. Oh! You are passing!

Things are ready. All
things, because something
must be settled. Slung.

Answering laughter. Mixture of
diamond and diamond
and blood, a rope of flowers.

TWO

At the back of the house, in bright
impermanence—conscious of being
not, but nearly, everything.

.

Barriers of green. When you have
all, why torment the depths? I'll
go. Sunburnt crater.

.

Before the laughter was heard, night
with its varied lights. Steal
out. Drink the cooling night.

.

Do not copy this wall, down
to the garden. I was faint. The lights
blinded me. I wanted the night.

.

First questions, signs not
from which quarter,
coming.

.

For a moment: empty. Abridging all
questions, until we reach all questions
cease. New tempo.

Immediately, eating it O in this
world, or one other—will you
(spins like fine gold) clamber over?
.

Into caressing shadows.
High walls, making possible high
wall, so precisely unrepeated.
.

Ivy-hung sculptured colonnade and
beyond. "As before a sepulchre."
Leap. Flesh tones like deity.
.

Not to be repeated. Near but un-
seen. Trickles and dances off.
Shadows of a shadowy pool.
.

Once again, endlessly, not
to be repeated. Unvanished if
substance. Into the voice.
.

Passion, breaking the orders it
so resembles. Darkness, like familiar
darkness, my lamented desert.

Poplars. Sycamores. Turpentine trees.
Circular benches of marble supported by
fabulous monsters. Imitation of a wood.

.

Sad at supper. Laughter always from
within. Here. Here. Hurry! Do
not be seen.

.

Soft strains enclose the garden.
Each sings through to the end.
Does not want us to yield blindly.

.

Stone floor in silver light, moon
playing also on the dancing rill. Stolen
sweets. Near the temple, overladen.

.

Stroll out upon the portico.
The very good we find or achieve seems
guilt toward some other world.

.

Such silence. Wind-driven
clouds. We collide with already
us. My life is full.

Summon the stranger. Silence of
apprehension. High wall, in constant
alteration, under the sun.

.

The voice you would prefer to
hear, where objects
disappear, as in a little window.

.

Thousands stand about the door, souls
walking in light, singing hymns of
night. Inconceivable unity.

.

Threads gathered up. Soaring toward
you or falling from you. Who
can begin again? Unravel.

.

To pass unrecognized toward your
hiding place, not sure what news
yawns in the same past.

.

Under a sense of sunlight about
to grant your desire.
You hear this madness?

Variations. Except, of
course, for slight—now
failing—reflections.
.

Whispered words, unspoken
thought. Loss of stern
ornament. In sleep, your heart:
.

You have not moved.

THREE

"I have trekked far," is the quiet reply. To which we should add that when it was all made—with such a perfect blending of love, secret enterprise, and malevolent cunning—it was left outside. The action seems to be wholly mysterious, as is fitting. We must reemphasize the complete independence of the author and his traces. Can we say that they are a "pathos"? an "image"? a "Nothing"? A breaking into the garden? Or a bridge? In any case, after this there is, for a time, no ghost in the stairwell, though a light appears in some neighboring window and goes out again.

FOUR

I

Fate is cleverer than the king
of Babylon. Shadows of yew
fall through windows onto

the floor of the nave and
touch the pillars with tattered
shade. You claim the dearest wish of your

life is to sink into a soul-freezing
situation of horror. The music of a crash
caught in the hollow of a wooded hillside.

2

Grave, questioning sweep—chiefly the weird
that arouses our keenest hopes. The garden of
dreams contains a summerhouse, hazy

period of my growth. There are bodies,
not greatly extended, called seas nevertheless,
because of their depth and

violence. I've some little
doubt about this ceremony entirely
embedded in a cup of grassy hills.

3

Pardon me for loitering. I was sleeping
soundly when I was roused by the loud
clang of what turned out to be

a large brass candlestick, flung
against the banister. Unprotected,
destitute of the means of self-defense, you

hug to yourself the consciousness of
vanished beauty. The sea is un-
certain, on the main and also along the coast.

4

Strange rooms. Through these experimental
years, who can describe beauty
in the dead of night? Complain of

frivolity or of portraits exactly
like ghosts. The waters of the great
surrounding sea will completely

evaporate when the sun opens the fifth
of its seven eyes. Oh yes, I take
pleasure in backgrounds, bringing them forward.

5

These are only a few of many
legendary details, called from the distant
future where each thing has its

end, including sea, sun, the eyes.
You live in another season—even now I
feel acrobatic instincts. Large strange

rooms. A silver cup from his household
plate, a sky of the same
gray tones, a great wilderness of books.

6

When the sea subsides into utter
calm, changing clouds caught in its
clarity, then fishermen say the sea

is thinking about itself. A dark back
room, looking down upon a narrow
courtyard—waking out of some

dream of specters, bellowing the most
frightful shrieks, forgetting only
at the sound of somebody's voice.

7

You light me to bed with your light, and
never a night but I am
prey to ghostly visions—a tenderness

not usual in my family. The lion
pauses a certain space of time, amid
a sea of divers thoughts, choppy half

desires, memoranda of search
and hunger, very peculiar
ideas of the world.

FIVE

after this, the cold more intense, and the night comes rapidly up

.

angels in the fall

.

around a tongue of land, free from trees

.

awakened by feeling a heavy weight on your feet, something that seems
inert and motionless

.

awestruck manner, as though you expected to find some strange presence
behind you

.

coming through the diamond-paned bay window of your sanctum

.

a crimson-flowered silk dressing gown, the folds of which I could now
describe

.   .

deathly pallor overspreading

.

describing the exact nature of your nightly troubles

.

discomfort at seeing a surface spoiled

.

echo and foretaste

the entrance blocked, not only by brambles and nettles, which have to
be beaten aside, but by piles of faggots, old boxes, and even refuse

.

expecting every moment to see the door open and give admission to the
original of my detested portrait

.

fantastic wigs, costumes, other disguises

.

filling up the width of the street

.

frequent tussles

.

the glitter of silver and glass and the subdued lights and cackle of
conversation around the dinner table

.

high-backed carved oak chair

.

I have omitted in my narration . . .

.

in a great raftered hall

.

in a tableau vivant, as an angel, sewn up in tights, with wings on your
back

.

light your candle and open the window

lines of your dress, with a hint of underthings

.

looking up, our problem still unsolved

.

luxurious with heavy silk and rich rococo furniture, all of it much soiled
with age

.

many questions about the stars, of which you gave me my first
intelligent idea

.

meanwhile, the snow, with ominous steadiness, and the wind falls

.

my weakness for the Ypsilanti Waltz, which I did regard as the most
wonderful of compositions

.

neat strip of fine turf edging the road and running back until the poison
of the dead beech leaves kills it under the trees

.

never venturing farther than a sandy beach, but losing everything at sea

.

not crawling or creeping, but spreading

.

not just out of repair, but in a condition of decay

.

only a foul trick after all

on the face of the judge in the picture, a malignant smile

.

profound impressions of unearthly horror

.

rambles and adventures among the rocky banks

.

the rope of the great alarm bell on the roof, which hangs down

.

rough horseplay and quarrels

.

sashes that splinter at a touch

.

the serpentlike form of the seraphim

.

something uncertain at work among the monuments

.

the thing on the bed, slowly shifting

.

till this particular day has passed through all the seasons of the year

.

the vicar, who used to tell us the story of *Robinson Crusoe*

.

waves and their whelps

while with a sickening revulsion after my terror, I drop half fainting
across the end of the bed

.

with a pair of great greenish eyes shining dimly out within the lattice
fronts

.

with painted carvings of saints and devils, a small galvanic battery, and a
microscope

SIX

Behind and above, I saw then everything
that was happening on earth and can
describe the hum of clouds. Why

are you screaming? East of the sycamore
is the other world. Look: the same
road, lisp and rustle. At length you

may come to no decision, straight
as a die. Ample time for
dancing between acts. I am relieved

the sycamore is healthy—at my
death I will go to it. Not
*in*to it—but someday, if sufficiently

sensitive, you may
spot me, in the guise of child or
dwarf perhaps, leaning against the trunk like

a fallen branch. We are talking with
rhyme and reason, an art of
shading, smooth gradation

of loud and soft, velocity
distributed. Self-love, seeking
an object, splits

us in two. Nothing is
hidden from us, hour by
hour, with absolute certainty of its

occurrence. If I do
show up (perhaps as
dwarf or child) it will be to

the west—or south of the tree, *facing*
west. Children still of tender age are
taken into the forest and none of them

dare go home again, more and more
unfit for work, spending precious
time and learning nothing,

cantabile. You behold the wind coming
up the street. I doubt the easiness of
any access. Witness the horrors

of original scenery. First a
river. Then
a hill. What do you

bring that is good? The dead
pick these flowers and place them behind
their eyes and drink this water and have

no more desire. Good country near
the church. Twelve coffins
filled with shavings and in each

the little death pillow. The air is at
rest, belting around. Nothing
left for us to think about. Everything

proclaims the same language, not
the same thought. French windows, open
wide, flood the room with

regular patterns, like a military
parade. A large hall to
contain them. Pleasure at

every step. Soldiers swaying in the
breeze, their abundance and their
freedom. Counterblow to

night. I must devour you—skin,
hair, and all. We must provide
for winter. Now let us examine

the dwellings of the kingdom
of heaven. What happens to
the severed parts? I hurl an ax

into the storm. Love potion: blood
dripping from the finger from one
year into the next. Hence my dread

of day's endless chain. When darkness
overtakes us, we will find no
shelter. I do not mind being

coachman on the box, but
drag you myself I
will not. Death is something

that occurs to a sleeper. Hair parted and
gathered in a Psyche knot back
of your head. Death

can strike the eye. Oh for me I
have other plans. Reason intervenes
to order impulse. Still, it

can appear—death—as
a solution, which of course
it is. Alone with your treasures,

hardly a budge to the little
ravine. Wild animals. Cry yourself
sleepy. I used to go to all

vampire films. Hope sprang
eternal. Lovers drink each
other's blood. First a river, then

a hill. A new vein opens. I
have admitted too many entities. Time
to razor down. I understand

how one might prefer to walk
bent over, eyes
to the pavement. We hear

horses neigh, soldiery laugh. Laid
waste, the farmers' fields. The cattle
killed. Men, women, slaughtered. Kings:

those that sleep. The king wears
a dragon mask. The king's soul
is lost and the king's soul is

found again. Dearest to each animal
its own constitution. Endless
causation. The king is not

what he seems to be. Death, disease,
weakness, being out of condition,
ugliness, and the like. If I

stir in my sleep, it is because the
point of a weapon has
touched us. It was my own

regard that quickened death, my
interest that made it personal.
Stories told by the fire at night making

creepy flesh, pneumatic
power, *cantabile*. You inspect
each one, lift it, put your

nose to it. Snow spreads a white
sheet over the grave. Will you
come? Verbatim. While wishing

still fulfills. Keep your eye
out for me, in the vicinity of
that tree. I will be

near it. Perhaps, in spring, as a child
reaching for the center. Look at the sycamore:
tall, healthy, flashing its regalia.

Falling in Love
through a Description

Such a love is a tumbledown building without any foundations.

IBN HAZM, *The Ring of the Dove*

for Françoise de Laroque

An Apparatus

From where I sit, I can see other
things: a silver porcupine, pins
standing upright. It is a vanished tale of a
vanished forest at the shore of a vanished ocean.

I call the dead as often as I can. In the
vaults, among mummies—this is pure
memorial. I am the girl in whose
eyes the name is written.

I feel as if veiled, as if soon I
shall get to know something. There are people
with encephalitis who cannot go
forward, but can go backward, and can dance.

In this rough draft of my memoirs, my brother
comes toward me—frightened, skeletal—longing
for marvels. I cannot describe it better than by
comparing it to other figures, intoxication.

Mere reflexes, as for instance breathing, can become
conscious. One of two rivals has his
ornamental tail bit off. In dying sounds, barely
reaching our ears, a melody continues.

No end to it—an infinite progression. All this
love of a bygone age. Watch the track
of a concentrated sunbeam through our lake ice:
part of the beam is stopped, part goes through.

Now the upper surface buckles, phantasmagoria of
unchained passion—under which the land
quakes, the ocean swells, and a myriad-years-
old forest snaps and cracks.

Surpassing all forms of experience, the wide, deep,
freshwater lake—on which the city
is built—rises before us. Here a modern idea
interposes, a new body made from the elements.

Then everything is forgotten. Sometimes thoughts
are cut off and sometimes they are the
blade which cuts. At the present gravel pit, electric
lights in the evening cast their magic blue sheen.

There's the sun, a crack above those
hills, breaking the day. If the door open, who
comes in? If it close, what will interrupt
my train?

The staircase effect supplies strong evidence
for a subjective map. Downhill, the sun
trickles, unperturbed. Here trots a mammoth with
red wool, through the black yew forest.

The tendency of elements to linger on: You say
I dream of what I want, but what I
want now is to dream. The cold rind
broken, the same wind blows.

Through a lens of ice, the dark
heat of the sun burns wood, fires gunpowder, melts
lead. Perhaps a cloud of musk arises, such as
issues from a crocodile in passion.

Unless light falls properly upon these
flowers, you cannot see them. All associations at
this level rain down from above. We
talk of word-pictures.

We observe vertigo. We reach the cleft
by a steep gully or *couloir*—very dangerous, the
path from the heights, the glory of
the prospect, the insight gained.

What I mean is a disturbance in
all the senses at once. You will not find
the flowers confused. Facing a certain
wind, there is always danger.

Apparent Motion

All noises, like the rattle of a train, seem
to speak. Miraculous birds. I know what it
is, but if I close my eyes it's
gone. A giant with no head, he
sees through his feet.

Apple-hung, not previously
imagined. Unwilled, not immediately
recognizable. Faces and figures
unknown, luminous, not logically con-
nected, in divers outfits and attitudes.

Exceptional losses for a hundred
years. A secondary forest. This causes
ships or icebergs to appear as
if inverted and suspended in the sky, with
nothing visible on the surface of the sea.

Flat. Dimmed. Everything
tastes the same. Ships idle in port. On
the other hand, sounds may be
louder, colors brighter, a red
roof like a flame.

Not just because I opened my eyes, but
because I tried to *see*—the foliage beyond
imagining. Fantasies of attacking or
being attacked. Wild animals race through
the closed door—slow, along the wall, to hide.

Psychotic children with fabulous
memories. Parts estranged or dead, commonly
the face, especially the mouth, the
arms and hands. I would shorten my
nights by wandering my creatures.

These are not outward, physical
eyes, neutral in tone, relatively
insufficient. Pictures jump about. Furniture
comes to life. Rushing sounds, bangs and
cracks. Ghastly—I do not know how.

While I read, the white page turns
red, the letters green. As if
through a veil, through
a wall, from far away, altered, two-
dimensional. Longing for sadness.

Competing Depth

As the wave reaches the church, it
separates right and left and the edifice
is embraced. Confabulation fills the gap.

Still, the sound-shadow is only partial. Errors
in recognizing the surroundings are
paralleled by misjudgments of time and trouble.

The pulse advances, squeezes the particles to-
gether. Meaningless patterns distorted,
so as to make them look familiar.

When a long sea roller meets an isolated
rock in its passage, it rises against the rock,
clasps it all around. Past events, pushed.

Excuse for Festivities

Alcove to alcove, to enjoy a variety
of prospects. A looming stimulus and the visual
cliff. Attack and exploration. Ill health and
fatigue play a part. Speed irrelevant.

Apocryphal stories cluster. Modesty above
personal enjoyment. Responses include, on the
one hand, crouching, curling up, taking
cover, and on the other, calling out, escaping.

First there is weariness. Then other causes of
forgetting. Then still others, and then there is
weariness. Fur elicits fear. Or a pair of
staring eyes or something falling from the sky.

Instant flight or, sometimes, catalepsy. In hot haste,
beating his charger with a furled umbrella picked
up by mistake. A quite unnecessary
withdrawal that evening. I detest drama.

Met by a sudden movement or mysterious
sound, few of us learn. Down a dark
passage, patting a dog or psychoanalyst,
comfort me with toy, charm, talisman.

Now I remember a party. Year passed into
year. I betook myself to a belvedere
overlooking a garden. Covering my face with
my hands, I can never recall that day.

One clue, universally known, is pain. Danger
has already materialized, experimental, hard
to extinguish. Safety may lie in one
special place or anywhere in the tops of trees.

The calming effect of contact. A response
learnt as the result of a single violent experience
does not die easily. Common sense doesn't
cover everything. In my youth, I was afraid.

There is no evidence available. From what I can
tell, things are beautiful in the eyes of their
admirers. The widow of Napoleon plays cards with
Wellington, and the coins they play for are napoleons.

The Fountain of Quiet

A feeling of smooth
functioning. Straight lines
are infinite and if I were
to follow one, there could be
no arrival. Water, stretched
till like a rope it
breaks of its own weight.

A genuinely restful
state—leisurely, con-
templative. Each element to its
natural level. Not a word
about physical properties. The earth
turns less and less quickly; day by
day, each day is longer.

A great deal of rain begins as snow, melting in its fall. There are many
accounts which we must accept or reject on their own merits—it being
impossible, through distance in time or other obscurity, to get behind the
report to a more factual view of things.

From infancy we remember nothing, or very little. Analysts insist on
explaining this—they go so far as to give reasons why we do not recall the
womb, which they suppose veritable Eden. They must not realize, what
seems obvious, that memory itself is learned. Pigeonholes are not all that
easy to come by—as, later, they are hard to demolish—and without them
nothing can be stashed away, let alone drawn out again.

Here on the rim of the basin, the spray—shifting as it does with every breath of wind—avoids me for a time and then flings its damp against me. It is not loud—the water spurting up, dispersing into foam, falling again lightly—but such noise as it makes, a high white plash, stills my internal chatter, covers over the fag ends of my thought where anxieties collect to murmur and mutter.

Oceans of spider silk. Various
materials, depending on the pressure
to be withstood. A doctrine of
movement. A doctrine of place. And
about fire. Allegedly underlying equally intelligible
disturbance. Comparatively little more than vacuum:
intrinsic beauty, gelatinous, infolded.

Order predominates, as Theophrastus noted, only in the heavens and in the heaven of mathematics. A slow influx of ideas may gather speed, like any natural course of things, flowing faster at the surface than along the bottom. The spray cools me, seems somehow to be listening—its sound so general, so unarticulated.

The glory of our midden: a long
trajectory of high-
tech debris. Copper, bronze, bored
stone. Tides in narrow
straits. Colossal sonic booms should
pervade the lower atmosphere. Lord
of Eternity, within thy ship . . .

There is a problem with trains of thought. They have to be stopped before they end as mere cadence, waves against the shore, clickety-clack, something solely for the inner ear. A delay is necessary at both transfer points: where a stone hefted is the stone's weight, and where the stone is—at a remove—the thing called stone.

The tendency of sprouts, against the
perpendicular. Ascending air
necessarily cools. Nothing can
happen which might not lead
to catastrophe. Unfree. Buffeted.
Vacillating. Live height of the
water. A theory of overflow.

Tuning between parts. Blue-black
of the sea. Isis on the Rhine. Isis on the
Danube. There is no doubt about this: ex-
citement caught, unable to spread, will find
some other tonal valley and
flow there like a stream. Extra-
cellular space. Succession of shapes.

Unclassified properties, patches of white, tend not to lie, as it seems they should, within their own dark outline, but appear larger than they are, projecting outside the supposed area, demanding other planes. So long as I am neither asleep nor at rest, I am occupied with something. A vapor goes up, little bubbles of water filled with fire.

The Growth of Private Worlds
from Unattached Feelings

Ambiguous words provide harmless
remarks. Suddenly things mean something quite
different. Transfigured faces. Harmless
laughter sounds like derision. A fire
breaks out in a faraway town.

Brilliant hair. Blowing. In the morning, I
run away. No direction. No
up or down. No dimension. Everything
happens quickly. A subtle, per-
vasive, and strangely uncertain light.

Conversation in a low voice through an iron
tube 3,120 feet in length. Eternal harmony,
practicing on silent violins. Fourteen times
lighter than air. Thus we distinguish
primary, nondirectional urge. Driven.

First, in default of anything better, with
a little tin cannon, the torn remnants of which are
now before you. We can compare it to a
photographic plate. Happiness contentless
but bright. Afterward, with pistols.

It is a pulse and not a puff. Specifically: in the
limbs, forehead, chest, or stomach. She hurts
in her breast and her abdomen, but it is
more a sadness. A progressive
series, subject to interruption.

Something is going on. The dead Arch-
duke is resurrected. Unusual
beauty of the landscape. I think the world
is turning around me. Whatever position we
take, space is not place.

The two men in raincoats, a few
steps away, are the priest Melchizedek and old
Doc Brinkley. Overpowering glory of the sun-
light. Menacing faces. Traps. Allusions. At
twelve o'clock, there are additional insults.

The world is changing. Odd words
picked up in passing. Scaffolding around
sound houses. Something is bound to
happen. A trail is blazing. Hold
on: there is always a farther step.

Under the voice. To and fro. And thus tardily
deliver up the motion. We shall fly straight
into the sun. Beware of starting small—everything
else may follow. Unbearable, because
it comes from within and will out.

Who first constructed a perfect violin? While
the wave moves forward through considerable
distance, each particular particle makes only
a small excursion. I myself have had objective
experiences, which I would not interpret.

Instances of Echoes

By day, seventeen syllables. Twenty by
night. An idea out of the blue. The whole
incident gives one a lot to think about: loss
of interest, lack of desire. She cannot move
mouth or limbs while praying. Something
takes possession of my head.

In the whispering gallery, the faintest
sound is conveyed from one side of the
dome to the other, but heard at no intermediate
point. The simple urge to move may
arise on its own. It is as if she
were dying. And the urge to do something.

Jump out of bed, thrash about, bite, run
against the wall. Mr. Wheatstone
finds a word once pronounced will be repeated
a great many times. A single exclamation
appears like a peal of laughter, while
the tearing of paper is like the patter of hail.

Often we cannot decide. It comes up her
body, right up to the neck, like
a hand. Sonorous waves reach
the air in succession. One. Two.
Three. And thus die away in the sweetest
cadences. She is stricken utterly.

Though they are fully conscious, they cannot move. The tick of a watch from one end of the church to the other. Inexplicable, sporadic, alien. The eyes are upturned, fixed. We are in the dark as to where the actual point of impact lies.

Internal Evidence

Dreadful firsthand descriptions of wounded
journeyings. Everything grows fleeting, vague,
loses its structure. Healthy people
often have hallucinations.

First thrill. Uneasy oil, as after
sunset. On a long journey by rail
we may doze, experience a low ebb of the
wave crest. Ambiguity. Enigma.

Maps not allowed. At the moment of waking,
a few incomprehensible words
remain. One can dream and be
an observer at the same time.

Over slippery roads in a Scotch mist to
deep meanings or the presence of
the infinite. I feel awakened by
order, but once I wake, it's gone.

Pedal creaks. Tone rotten. Much more difficult
to concentrate on anything, contemplate
anything, think of anything. The peak of
clarity lies in the middle. Liszt, etc.

The alleged spy reports himself once a
day at noon. This suggests a state of over-
wakefulness. All that is left is
a handful of psychic fragments.

Through a street of villas, tennis lawns close-
fisted. Do we find abnormal alertness, ab-
normal norms? I bring the book
near my eyes. I cannot drink it.

Trumpeters covered with gold braid and with
black velvet jockey caps. Another scene
follows one. I must have been asleep a
long time, when I realize I am dreaming.

Vast wool warehouses. An empty
consciousness, which we can
interrupt at will. Thinking de-
finitively pigeonholed. Images derailed.

An Involuntary Winter

All the accustomed stages of love. Fear
of the dark resembles fear of
animals. Veering a tad to the left,
away from suburban streets. Deep emotion.

I can predict unpleasant
events, though fear of pain
is rarely mentioned. Veiled ladies in
guarded palaces, exchanging letters.

If it were possible to understand
the danger of falling, without the experience of
falling, its manifest effect
on the soul. Hidden in the sleeve, anxiety.

The sacrifice intended is eventually
held elsewhere. Purely imaginary picture
of the person whose veil is kept constantly
before the mind. Messengers to and fro.

The voice of a girl singing
behind a wall. Startle, crying, and
diffuse movements. I've a constitutional
nervousness on the subject of fires.

Without actual sight of the object
of affection. Sprawling about on
sofas, dressed in indecent clothes. Mark
in your memories this sleeplessness.

Leeway

A brown rock jutting: phantastic
citadel. A wind-cursed olive
stretches above a ridge. I would like to discuss
many things. Picture this emptiness.

And when it is autumn, then spring
is here already. The trees conspiring: come,
let us make war against the sea. Love
wanders, overlooking a wheat field under the snow.

Even the next five minutes do not
lie ahead. Towers, like a temple, white
marble piercing the blue. It feels
always, again, like the same moment.

Smaller. Larger. Or aslant—space
with an atmosphere. The present only an
anecdote. Something in the wall stirs,
the wallpaper thrives. I am still seeing the room.

Suddenly the landscape, sometimes there, sometimes
here. Darkness inside the body. Then
the veil drops. Everything so quickly, walking
faster. Belated dreamer on granite cliff.

Sylph, bathed in moonlight: new organs
of love. We will return to this
subject. Disturbance forgotten, and hardly to
be compared with what we ordinarily call time.

Long Terms

I've lost my way on
more than one occasion. In some
temporary form, the question seems
important. A momentary act of
awareness and then.

Suppose I listen to
common sense, unable to recall
events immediately preceding. Suffering
"reminders" throws
no light.

What you learn while drunk
is best remembered when
drunk. I cannot even think
time in reverse. Retention
better after sleep.

Working backward, learning
to learn. I cannot see how the birth of
Jesus, for example, makes "now"
indispensable. A diversity
above zero.

Looming

Afraid of a jack-in-the-box, sudden
approaches, loud voices, mere
strangeness. Your room still darkened and you
still on the couch. Above all, fear
of the dark. And in the dark, alone.

Fear of calamity—fire, flood,
murder—allows the vaguer
anxieties to settle. In this house, nothing
green survives. Fear
as a matter of taste.

Fear of gold rims, wrinkles, or an unexpected
noise. Attacked or overwhelmed by
an object rapidly advancing. Indian
file, toward the spiral staircase. Frightened,
thinking you just might go.

Fear of strangers. The plant you
left me, in its tinsel-wrapped
pot—two days later it
died like a discovery. Fear
of illness, damage, death.

Wariness. Distress. Terrible confessions
of past crimes, shocking proofs, or secret
wickedness. The upper hinge gives way. We wander
one garden after another. Glad rather than
ill, maybe, from this loss of memory.

"Majesty"

Among other economies, I'm of two
minds, one possessed, the other
a deep peace. Violent trembling
seizes me, launched in the interval.

Enemy of children, of quaint little
things, of jokes and pictures. Enemy
of comic papers and caricatures, of
water-drinking. Too short for tragedy.

Rarely has a large or distant expedition
ever succeeded in its object, as may be
seen in the failure of foreign missions, of
human development, the immediate phenomena.

Sympathy for the victors, who gallantly
perish. Collateral catastrophes, as if they
had a will. The more distinctive visual images
sail too long, relinquish, burst.

The "inner voice" is playing a game. Eagerness
and obstinacy. A mysterious invisible
placed in the mouth. We know too well how
terrible it is to contend against personality.

The whole idyll vanishes. Southward along
a coastline, down among cities. Across the
gulf to the promontory. Probably
astonished. Not without mistrust.

You are now my prisoner. Physically I am
myself. Cultivated living, good manners, rich
food and drink, order and elegance in
my house. Erect military bearing.

The Minimum Visible

Between the appearance of any
two ideas. Must
set the clock. Previously
future events. A little way back behind
moments. The spirit of a hawk.

In the future, the case
is altered. Intelligent trees
observing such a world the
sapling grows smaller. Gross
observation. Openly in full cry.

Successive acts in the direction
of the arrow. A short stretch already
past. Nothing in my direct
experience what is wrong?
This kind of trap survives.

Taking or has taken place
must be false, the narrow
now. Relived. Take-for-
granted may explode. Less:
thrash the wings.

Urging two senses at once suppose
I listen to a drum a two-second
glissando they have any
bearing on our normal ex-
perience. Recall the hounds.

Within interval of physical space the
theory elusive. Con-
founding pulsational. Hold
the pendulum. Trail. The hollow
shaft of the feather.

Misfit River

A wide expanse. In the short winter
days of the campaign, eternity
sings like ocean swell. Most suicides
in May, June, July. Unusual
heat drives the soul toward God. A
cul-de-sac. Vocalizing the remoter
arpeggios.

Dark strain of a lover's
lament. Made by percussion
alone. There is someone
shouting from the housetops and
no one listening to all the secrets
broadcast down. You call me
out of the night.

Formulas preserved, verbatim, in
a language no longer comprehended. Where
doors are all on the left. Sacrament
of now. To make the elixir, but
make it with none of the usual
ingredients. Pointing straight upward like
naked fingers.

Somewhere. Somehow or
other. What remained of winter, when
winter was over, close to the ground, collecting
around roots of plants here and now
springing. Each stage several
million years. A process of removing
bark from trees.

The descent from the summit
abrupt. A common house. Alongside my
days, the metaphysical day
extends, stretches of
unfathomable. That heaven and earth
affect mankind doubtless true, but
painful to measure.

Momentary Whole

A bear. What does he eat? A feeling of
being spun around until figures appear.

Bang. Smash. The bus crashes into
another bus. A hellish dazzle.

Compression in the head. Attacks of
rage. Whispers. The conductor cries, "All aboard."

Deep clouding. Around the focal point a field
spreads, dimming toward the periphery.

Distraction by voices, hardly perceptible. His head
falls in the ocean. The vortex willy-nilly.

One of his shoes off. Two of his
socks off. Single words like "power" or "life."

Praying. Mumbling meaningless phrases. Eats
a boy and a fish. Eats sand and a shovel.

Spiders fly around. Saying a prayer makes the
voices go. Faraway places where demons attack.

Threatening figures tower over us. Run very
quickly, because the cars are coming.

Words for inner protection. The works
have stopped. Lost thoughts. I overestimate hours.

Natural Bridge

Climbs on the first spider that
comes along. Sees himself distinctly
on the same road, riding toward. Strange
peace of mind. Land of Commotion.

Enlarges, gets stronger, heavier, and along with this
the pillows get bigger. Earth as it was, without
railroads, the Eiffel Tower, the Suez Canal and
with the Island of Krakatoa, before 1883.

Feels he is a soap bubble, or that his limbs are
made of glass, or describes himself in
countless ways. Dreams of icy satellites
on ancient extinguished suns.

Like a doll from Nuremberg. Head floating free,
half a mile behind. Systems no telescope
can resolve into individual stars. Exceptionally
three-dimensional and highly detailed.

Prefers the thick tangle of some
dwarf shrub. Affirms that another
person lies on his left side in the same
bed and wants to push him out.

Strips of light, spiraling like a tenacious
climbing plant. We possess, from this
period, pictures of animals, diluvial and
characteristic. New heaven and new earth.

The walls are simple, white, unornamented. In long
cases along these walls are dark stone
fragments, resembling broken animals. Terrible
teeth. Blood of grapes and mulberries.

What new impetus in the millions
of space and time? Provokes the elephants to
fight. And for every elephant a
thousand men. So decorated, at such expense.

Night Soil

A random walk, its ordinary motion
blurring chronology. Behind, a
seascape. As if on a ship's deck.

Fear of defeat is an old habit. All this fuss, with my
hat pushed back. Honeyed phantastic. En-
raptured soul. Another blow.

From the end of the corridor, at the kitchen
window. These frosts are cruel. I am not
up to them. Out on the balcony, basking.

History is trash. Elaborate battles make
peace and then, after spectacular defeat,
I may go and I may not.

I'm in a bad mood, forever. We bring no
resemblance. Torment and dreams. Grotesque and in-
clement. Always the same amazing luck.

Rest before the fireplace, forget
fine spacing. To control noise by
attacking the odds. Grope for the knob.

Shutting out light and air. Cold stone
floor. Sinking. Devouring
pit. Dissolve, now, the dungeon.

Streaks of light stream from your
shadow. Redisposed. Clouds are not
simply carried. We observe words and winds.

The door slams behind us. Not so much
forced by the sun as simply
coasting under our own inertia.

The knives of reality. Repeat the names.
Doves, when they fight. Scorn is best and
yes, we may go and we may not.

Plurality of Worlds

And each inhabited. And each
inhabitant resolves. And I, I with
my various processes. I stumble, I
revolve.

As one
sees, in the desert, water
welling, always distant, forever
unapproachable.

A view of the chase
from the battlements. To see something—any-
thing—I always step back. And then:
where am I?

Distant. Unapproachable. My
name. Jericho. Absurdly—I mean, out of
tune. And forgetfulness? deceit?
error?

For us to grow
old, the moon must rise. From invisible
fire, flames leap into view. A dream
of bodily heaven.

Hot colors, subtle
nuances. Motives recast in site
after site. Figures absorbed by
a plethora of drapery.

I must remove all this:
evening chill, an impression of transparency, your
presence—remove it all, without
letting anything go.

I was born in December
and things seem always to come at me like
January. The fifty-third bird in the
tree this morning.

Joy, laughter,
lamentation—it's like a map. Minuet.
Waltz. Ninety percent too
dark to see.

Let me think now. Roads.
Tombs. Temples. I could list my
Friends . . . What will I
forget next?

Light, analyzed by
dusk, and then? The specters
still there. A painterly softening. Almost
heraldic poses.

Long narrow
slits of light, dark bars against bright
ground, or straight-line borders peculiarly
oriented.

Looking one way, everything
is lost. The other direction: nothing to
lose. In a crystal I glimpse, maybe, my
waking state.

My soul's
fictitious body . . . Think. My
health: the world's long
lingering illness.

Pain, hot-cold, mere
contact. Crude sensory modalities. These
remain after destruction of the sensory
cortex. Pain.

Shock waves. Feathery
feet of barnacles. It does not
reach us, the sun's bottomless
profundo.

Things age and, when old
enough, no longer able to resist,
become animate. Unable to stay
free of life.

What remains of
ancient rites? Grammar. I
would never give up anything I have, in
return for mere certainty.

Pointless

Cannot be aroused. Into the bright
light of day, where even no
tender shadow falls. Florid events.

Damp bench just under the ivy hanging
from the balustrade of the terrace. Dreamy
perplexity. Very few sensations appear.

Indescribably beautiful, with the colors
of springtime. Perceptions dim as
memories. Chilled and saddened.

Love, tenderness, triumph, ardor for war—nearly
the same emotions, but weaker, less complex, felt
by birds. Suggesting, continually, physical movement.

Nothing can be remembered. Has she
forgotten him? Difficulties in
reflection and subsequent amnesia.

The act of thought no longer. Frightened
by recent rain, all psychic events
slowed down and much more difficult.

Things which we advance along steadily, things
to be followed from end to end. Just
now, as I dream it, all.

Poorly Grounded Notions

And an inability to comprehend the
flow of time. We need only think of statements
by everybody. I cannot call my-
self myself. Up to this point, the dreamer
is dreaming, but now his dream
begins. Unities of recollection, separate
from one another. Thus in this present
world, there are different injuries.

I never hear them. They come
uninvited. Silver tissue. Garlands
between them. Any activity may produce
music. Aware of their existence as an
awareness of losing their sense of ex-
istence: vague, general, nameless, like
a nothing or the absolute. I am dead. I am
not alive, a music of exceeding shrillness.

May be pleasantly illustrated in the
following way. Light on his head. Felicitous,
contains some fabrication. I am
forced to shout out, trace failure to the stage
when plans are construed. I see a table
before me. I am reminded of another
table. I place table beside table. Separate
worlds. In what sense are we talking?

Real Motion

Keep well in mind that it is strangely possible
for us to oppose ourselves. An illustration: competing
visual fields. The projection room dark. The blue of the
sky would not move us, were it a foot or so above
our heads. Fear drives the body, looking for itself.

Someone lying in the roadway. About pain, we are
all more or less agreed, but reflection is
necessary for such functions as urination, walking,
writing, sexual intercourse. A single, unified
judgment establishes the matter as undecided.

Sweeps of the eye traverse and surmount
something, the traversing and surmounting of which
might, in another way, be a matter of time, toil,
danger—its very height suggesting the
violence of a fall. I am myself, but I develop.

The Sea-Fight Tomorrow

Afraid to take a chance. They
pass haphazardly in all directions.
Diving into his car. Or yours.

Are there no strangers in town?
Entering, leaving, crossing. I
cross to the window and wave.

Everybody looks alike. Pyramids.
It must be somebody who
has a house in the country.

He said he would. Characteristic
kinesthetic and tactile deficits on opposite
sides of the body. Something clicked somewhere.

It's got to be airtight on
the other end. The butterfly-shaped
central gray. Who is this man?

It was a restful ride. The transition
gradual, without sharp
demarcation. The house was full of pictures.

The night man was gone. Important
changes from level to level. I
pretend to listen.

Silk

Below a certain intensity of light, colors fade to black and white—or, rather, to gray. Things are best seen then—if we can resist the natural impulse to fix directly on them—out toward the periphery, where rods far outnumber the sparsely scattered cones. But they are vague and their color is gone. In the spectral twilight, my dark-adapted eyes find stars—lost again if I try to look at them.

Completely submerged. So quickly
injured and obscured by dust, phan-
tastic worlds, simultaneously. Irregular.

Daydreaming of fabulous wealth, castles,
foundations of cities. Disturbances
set it in vibration, so naturally.

Deprived by darkness of the decor I supposed essential, I find it after all not so absolutely necessary. Instead of panning across the things that are, I wait. And moments, one after another, pass in review, steadily, with an air of inevitability.

Double nature, extremely
elastic. The longer I look, the
stronger the enchantment.

From what I see, see at this particular moment, I turn, bringing to mind everything invisible, the rest of the world, my small view's vast remainder. I regard it all—as if by some strange geometry all lines crossed just at the point of my perception—not merely as unknown, but somehow, in its entirety, forgotten: an amnesia almost universal, its only flaw the small shard of my awareness.

I had thought objects essentially gray, sculpted in black and white—only that sunlight threw over them a mirage of color. Lately I have seen the grisaille of landscapes in moonlight also as a veil, covering untouched and incalculable volumes.

It is hard for us—creatures of surface—to reckon with depth, whether of earth or ocean. Under our feet, out of the air and the light, life is unimaginable—though we know perfectly well how waters heave with animals and plants and how the organic extends into the soil, deeper than the roots of the tallest trees.

Legs about twice as long as
the body. In the grip of powerful
entities. Sedentary under stones.

Objects around me, I take as elements of a vanity, but the dark of evening breaks them down into something less neutral: shadows issue odd invitations from surfaces blank by daylight. As edges more and more fail to separate, things unfocus and my distractions thin into less than air.

Persecution, blissful tranquility, lack
of coherence. Loops of a hackled band. Con-
cealed from sight, but in position.

Rarely seen but conspicuous, surrounding
retreat. Phases and crises. Long periods of
hell, purgatory, fragmented situations.

Swallows (and, I suppose, bats, could we see them against the dark sky) serve as barometer, rising to the level of their insect prey, as it rises with the falling weight of air, higher and higher toward downpour. Somewhere in the spiral of stars, there may be clouds of growth and decay, heavy with sensation, pulsing outward from no center. Immemorial processes throb behind any glance.

The world extends—its utmost space—from the spinal cord into the lower brain. Time, the cortex, grants us moments, one by one, in which to scan, facet by facet, the little that appears.

Uncanny import, vague riddles. Monday does not
rally. I sing. I count to 12,000. I see
other figures, dead and living, four kinds of silk.

Velvety black. Submerged in ex-
perience, with senses full, but
usually the visual. Lead-colored tinge.

Soft Hail

Afterward, to tell how it was possible to
identify absolute space, a matter of great
difficulty, keeping in mind always
that not all old music is beautiful and
therefore it's necessary to choose. Ice
loading and unloading as the ice caps
wax and wither. Brutal and uncouth from the beginning
even unto time, space, place, motion.

How are we to obtain true motion? I
predict a fiasco—and a fiasco
with catcalls. Wind circulation in the
case of plants, predators in the case
of animals, affecting their distribution on
the ancient land masses. And
who will conduct the chorus and
orchestra? Many things exist at once.

Predilection and preference. Begin
with the storm. A very agile, beautiful
voice. With tremendous temperament. The earth's
magnetic field weakening. Even the princess
is drawn into the violence of the action,
extremes of joy, mad ravings, almost
requiring the conventions of opera. Thus,
thus; we parted, thus to meet again.

Thus in a ship, under sail, since the sun
itself is moving, supposing Infinite
Space to be (as it were) Sensorium
of the Omnipresent. Reduced to a
few feet of ground, we begin with great
delight to plant a garden. The Czar is in
that garden. Quiet eruptions, safe enough to attract
tourists. We suppose other bodies annihilated.

Upon any conditions supposed, taught to describe
accurately, I detest everything that smells
of theory. If we look at similar
coral reefs, the past location of the same
precise environment can be traced. But
there the comparison breaks. And from these
relative motions will arise the relative
motion of a body on the earth.

Terrestrial Casket

Anything will do, but this is not wisdom, not a sage abandoning. No, some things I've learned, but even those I don't understand. Indeed, the more I know, the less it seems I comprehend.

At the point where it overcomes me and also at
the end. At any time of day. Another
set of experiences, real perceptions
misinterpreted. Detached, passive, even
indifferent. Such connection as there
is will predominate in confused sequence.

Day's shadow rising, I realize, a traveler by night. If you read this, do not be embarrassed at skipping the difficult parts. With so many people around, I hesitate to speak out loud and am looking for someone to deliver some lines.

First smell of dawn: strange
noises are heard, soil for
experiences. Fall of matter into
the clutches of what happens, with
terrific results: vivid scenes, landscapes,
crowds, graves. Actual approach.

Sad songs cover up crying. From Sheep Gut Slope one can see the Milky Way, like bones strewn across a dark plain. Sudden news, after millions of years.

The planets can hardly
keep in touch, dimming as night begins to
crumble. Half-sleep. Suffocated. I
dreamt it. Extinguished, the
zodiac, receding, the center
of light. Dreamt. Like lamps.

The Visual Cliff

Outside the town, or so placed
as to be isolated. Approached by wide
roads—there should be no inter-
ference with traffic or with the railway
system. An impervious surface, disinfected.

The floor must be made of jointless
paving, so that the earth is not
fouled in the process. The walls cemented
to a certain height above the floor—easily
cleansed. And prevent blood escaping.

The most convenient shape of the site
is a rectangle or square, one side abutting
on the principal road. Much depends upon design
and details of construction: adequate
lighting, ventilation, walls, floors, fittings.

Up a winding viaduct, by which in certain
houses, they reach the roof. Along the trolley line
to a place where. Narrow alleyway. In
subsequent passage. Driven. A house
on the river. An expert with the poleax.

Wandering Curves

A new ridge spreads underneath. Volcanoes, often
active, rim the Pacific. It bears little
resemblance to human behavior. She
crushes it in her hand and wipes it
across her sorrowful brow. Two
families of curves, drawn on a surface.

Such tremendous movements on the
surface must arise from internal
forces. Demoniac rage and
the traditional laugh of abandoned
villainy. My eyes fill with tears, my
knees double under me.

The weather is always important in
melodrama. Space is a function of
matter and energy—or, rather, of their
distribution. But how did we get like this—so
suddenly? *Despair sits brooding the putrid
eggs of hope.* The world's deepest earthquakes.

Under sustained pressure, even granite
flows. The whole of Scandinavia's
still rising, having been long depressed
by an enormous ice cube. The water behind
Boulder Dam is heavy enough to
ooze the crust along the mantle.

Will to Will

An interesting case, the progress of a bird. When
they move, they move quickly, a glittering
line. One's own performance can alter.

As a mere form or fold of the atmosphere, were
our organs sharp enough. I am, as
if I were not. Tendency to telescope.

A thought vanishes and there, before
sunset, someone else is thinking it. A note in
music, as the ordinary accompaniment.

But again, I have this encouragement,
not to think all these things utterly
impossible. Purchase new clothes, buy food.

Desperate attempt to escape perplexity. On the
surface too deeply absorbed to conceal
her ignorance. A cowboy leaves the ranch.

Four distinct things are to be borne in
mind: the square, a small body, free
air, the intensity. Went to town.

Mad. Foolish. The sound of an
explosion is propagated as a wave. Nobody
knows him, he's so dressed up.

Not particularly striking. The dog runs to him and
licks him. Reflected like light, refracted
like light, like light condensed by suitable lenses.

Stamp on the air the conditions of
motion. Sing a hymn in the passage, but
sing *so badly*. Haunting tune, idea, phrase.

The dog barks at him when he comes out. He
sells the cow, shops for a wife, builds
a new barn, buys cows. The rest I'm forgetting.

The Plummet of Vitruvius

for Peter Gizzi

PLUMMET

Altars

Should be lower than
the statues so that those praying must
look up. Their height
may be adjusted.

The Theater

Spellbound, my
pores open—into which
winds find their way. It takes
many days to chant the poem.

Voice is a flowing
breath, endless
circles like the increasing
waves in water, spreading until
interrupted.

When they are interrupted,
the voice breaks.

The Acoustics of the Theater

At what pitch the voice
begins, shifts, appears
stationary—as happens in singing, each
footfall music.

The gods enter to
sudden thunder. The morning
comes where the voice has a
gentle fall, throne to
throne, not
driven back.

The fruit of long
years, suddenly,
in an impulse of rage.

Perfect in sweetness after
twenty years of
loneliness. Sounds of indistinct
meaning check, as they sink
down, the rise
of succeeding sound.

On Climate Determining Style

Walking is healthy, particularly
for the eyes. Green things
give a clean-cut image, clearing away
gross humors. Misty vapors
never arise underground but
sidestep forward toward
the sacred fire.

Baths

Clay mixed with hair.

Retaining Walls

Plantations between colonnades—and I
must not omit the usefulness
of harbors. Then, on the water's edge, no
definite limits. Beyond the
stars of the Great Bear, to
disturb ancient pastures and the grassy
knoll: heaps of earth, broken wood, up-
turned sod, a
musical instrument.

The eye does not always
give a true impression, leading
the mind to judgment. In
painted scenery, for instance, I
cannot grant you anything.

Quantities of sweetmeats, cakes,
puddings. So
ashamed: from bodies
come undulating images thrown
into commotion. And the neighbors
are unkind.

Darkened windows, high
walls, confined spaces, unavoidable
obstructions, symmetrical relations,
not unlike beauty.

Natural Colors

With regard to
the point of sight and the
divergence of visual rays, a faithful
representation is
given, though drawn on a
flat facade: some parts
withdrawing, others
standing in relief.

First prize to the poet who
least pleases his audience.

Let the kitchen be warm.

Let oxen face only the direction of
sunrise and not
pass in envious silence.

Something happens.

Floors

The broken stone with its
bedding, rammed down hard.

Bring on your gangs, wooden
beetles, a solid
mass when the beating is finished.

On top, sift powdered
marble and lay on
lime and sand.

Spanish broom, silk cord, Greek
reeds pounded flat. Check any
drops that fall from the wall.

Below the Earth

My first glance takes in
an army, tens of thousands ready
armed. As a mirror reflects
indistinctly and with a feeble
light, so it cracks and
soon fades. From its surface a clear
image of the beholder.

In these paintings: harbors, promontories,
shores, rivers, fountains,
fanes, groves, mountains, flocks, and of
course shepherds. Sometimes mythological
episodes, figures of the gods, the
battles at Troy, wanderings of Ulysses.

Scorned in these days of bad taste.

Now we have frescos of mon-
strosities, candelabra supporting
shrines, stalks with human heads.

Malachite green, Armenian
blue, red earths in
abundance, vermilion like a drug.

Cinnabar

Certainly very strange. During
digging, under the blows, it sheds
tear after tear.

As a fire hidden in a
cave spreads outward, then
comes a scene of weeping.

Quicksilver

Four pints will be found to weigh
one hundred pounds. Crushed in iron
mortars, it keeps its
color—but is
spoiled by rays of the sun or the moon.

Immense elephants, rushing
furiously down, as
wonderful to the careful observer as
anything in nature.

This results in a color even
more delightful than ordinary black.

How to Find Water

Easier if there are springs.

Before sunrise, lie down flat where the
search is to be made. Place
chin on the earth, so that your
sight will not range
higher than it ought. Then
dig.

Valleys receive rains most
abundantly and snow
is squirreled by forests. Springs
run underground and
burst forth in the middle of
plains, protected
by the shade of trees.

Melting, it filters through
fissures in the ground and this
reaches the foot of the
mountain, from which gushing
springs come belching out. The earth
gives moisture under the influence
of heat, as a body emits sweat.

Taste.

THE UNRELIABLE NARRATOR

A great crime: she has
plunged a dagger into the heart
of her mother.

Strange.

The strangest thing: a mocking little pride with
a sinister click as of a fitting together of bad
pieces.

Beyond knowing. The mesmerist's only
child. A certain indication of anemia, too much
candy, and her charming eyes.

A privilege to be near her. My
inspiration. I risk an approach, what I call "the light of
day." Movements, with perfect indifference, turn
pale and shrink. *One
might have seen less:* the glimmer of
nothing. I caught no full-blown
flower of theory. And yet such visions pale in
flight.

Gorgeous, the domestic manufacture
of sausages.

Swallow and "so calligraphic a bird."

Somebody in Dickens. Attaching
diminutive eggs.

A glamour of memory.

Assurance of intimacy on the
summer air.

Nothing to explain. *We
needed breathing time.* Enough to
laugh. Odd what a difference. Only to
whistle to her. Delighted to come.

I know. Prepared to reply and turning a thick skein of
sewing silk sus-
pended in
entanglement. Shown "the faintest far-off
chords," *I ask myself.*

Our doom complete.

The difference, so simple: she had
folded up her manner. Great advantages now, my
dear, if he will show you. Dis-
appointment and its train might enter.

The wedding day, the fever season. But
they're dying. Kindred circle of the
tipsy, come to call. Lurid *memory*
remained with me, was indeed our sense of
"dissipation." (Horses. A high aesthetic revel.) Rome
made him invest unconscionable sums in postage. He
received answers in a delicate hand or *tried to think.*

Sublime synthesis. A bridge
over—liable to rear up. You just had to
wait for it, curiosity worked up with
a hard-boiled egg and a doughnut.

(Very ugly, but
I LIKE UGLY. Just the
sort of ugliness to
be *like looking*.)

Happy, he entered the streetcar's
nocturnal "exercises," the platform it evidently
was to be. *Bad lecture-blood* her enthusiasm. Catchpenny
monsters. *The ideal day* with that sense of resorting.

In imagination, we mean to do well. No faith in girlhood, her
    antediluvian
theories not much better. *Well,* she should get
rid of him. The logical hero.

CARRIAGE
—A TRANSITION—

|
|
|
|
|
|
|
|
|
|
|
|
|
|
|
|

Alien and I must
go home
|
|
|

All roads here cross no
end of small bridges creep
along dawn's crack
|
|
|

Another's night oblique
prison

|
|
|
The antagonists
(see it grows
dark around them) they
cannot fight much longer
|
|
|
Arguing
from illusions
|
|
|
Artificial night I want
to go who leaned against
the column
|
|
|
As I move toward
them into them they
thin allow me
no resistance so hard to say to
what extent I enter which
in which out

|
|
|
And an assembly of rarities a little Indian
bird phosphorescent by
night a snail that has
crawled on the Great
Wall of China a calico-
printer with the head of Cromwell
|
|
|
Bloody colors beggaring
description
|
|
|
By devious paths inwardly
fretting I crave
permission to make my
entrance on
the whim of the scene
|
|
|
Calamities may be
foreseen but there is
greater calamity they

appear the more
striking from being in immediate
antecedence (bright
colors cheerful
confidence gaudy stew) hell-
broth boiled in a
mess with potatoes onions
leeks my excursions
desperate

|
|

|

Dead instrument I
make no sound

|
|

|

A decline from river to
brook from brook
to ditch and
from ditch to drain

|
|

|

The deeps shallow and satisfaction the
ghost of desire

|
|

|

Dim view of a watery
plain
|
|
|
Dragged along the world's thin
line I reach as if to clutch
time in its passing
|
|
|
Earth now between
|
|
|
And Ellen Dawson and a
physician named Hands and
the gray horse in the stable
with sores on its flanks please
regard all this merely
effort of memory
|
|
|
Exchange of various
airs distant
lands and spices

|
|
|
The existence of
places is at stake
|
|
|
Follow those tracks along
what was once higher
ground luxuriant
tropical forests e-
vaporate to sandy
desert thick deposits of salt
and potash traps
for oil
|
|
|
(Go on with your terrible
tale but give
the right addresses)
|
|
|
A great black cauldron boiling over a
fire on the floor promises
better things an odor
permeates the vault

|
|
|
The horses in their stables
|
|
|
Hours later flying past
trees poles cross
streets and I'm
still it seems in the station
|
|
|
How many theories
end with one single but
insoluble ontological problem
|
|
|
I live at a distance
|
|
|
Imprisoned by laughter or
tears or tired
|
|
|

In the shadow of the tree piles
of little boxes I will put the house
here the ancient
climate disin-
clined derives whatever interest it may
have from what might
come to be like oh
frozen north the crab's
claws concomitants of shape
|
|
|
I open my hand the
wind as Sappho
felt it
"downrushing"
|
|
|
I preserve my
language
among sailors I
sing this song from
beginning to end
|
|
|

It is not in my power to
give the reader any
account of pleasure
information
talent
the thread (where I
broke off yesterday) the short dry
cough an understated cough
by no means specifying a
head perturbed with
brandy and fear
|
|
|
The King of Light a
closed eye river
to its source follow it back-
ward dust of water
|
|
|
Leave the
portrait forsaken
outline
|
|
|

Lifeless glove
|
|
|

Like the hoist of a flag to
produce unlikely design
|
|
|

Little waves breaking
against the summit it can't
be done real objects perceive
similarity though it
does not persist
|
|
|

Long argument or
short they tend to the same end a
kind of stream
dividing
a breathlike
stream
all rivers
|
|
|

Money will buy most things but
the train backs slowly such a
wild night
|
|
|
Mountains
airplanes
bodies out-
side the frame
|
|
|
My gravity distorts
the neighborhood every
quality adrift rub
the panes roar
of escaping steam
|
|
|
My house my
garden even the subjects
of the photos on
the wall
|
|
|

Night squandered on a streetlamp
|
|
|
Note how motives are re-
cast in situation after situation the
dancers fast the musicians
slow at the same tempo
|
|
|
No trains running come
many a week and as for
trees
|
|
|
Once it appeared to me
in the body or
out the senses
like children
|
|
|
One brief example our
interglacial
period scratch marks left
from boulders dragged across Laurasia or
Gondwanaland

|
|
|
Pillow for my head
|
|
|
A scherzo in a morgue
|
|
|
Simplest destruction
|
|
|
Spring unexhausted
shadow of
living light
|
|
|
Stricken
country submerged waste
|
|
|
Succession of shapes from the blue-
black of the sea

|
|
|
Such difficulties in the
idea of pose signs hang
over portable cities
|
|
|

The terrible fears almost
December over-
whelm me
|
|
|

There is no flesh under
the pictured dress not even
representation of
flesh oils bound
to primer
color
line
depth
|
|
|

There will be things to see chimney
lying in the road beer still in
barrel braces yet behind between
two kinds of being
|
|
|
These various names denote
the same person
|
|
|
Thinking of you I grow
old but would grow
old in any case
|
|
|
 (This view of the journey
moralized
fails to provide disorder)
|
|
|
Today warmer
than today
|
|
|

To the awful description of this
distemper I am not in-
sensible
|
|
|
Two tidal bulges undular or
breaking facing
moon and away from moon
granted a man carrying a
lantern bent
double against
the wind not
tonight
|
|
|
Up a winding drive of considerable
length at last to a broad open space
almost like a platform
|
|
|
Walking across someone
else's farrago (confused
world) an un-
bounded capacity for pain

|
|
|
Wandle
Falcon
Walbrook and the Fleet we
would be gold if
we had time
|
|
|
Waves high
dark without medium sinking
into the harbor
|
|
|
Whatever music
here at whatever tempo on its
way charges through
scratches and dust
|
|
|
What is left to leave out
|
|
|

And when I see this
layer of clouds and
other things the light I see
local
|
|
|
Window into the
dark very
dark indeed
|
|
|
Without sight
angel of my
consolation living
sapphires and rubies
|
|
|
You learn the grammar
then your nature
wild with rage
|
|
|

Zeno must have been
wrong since time's arrow has flown from
him to me
and is flying and
yet sometimes his argument
gives me pause
|
|
|
|
|
|
|
|
|
|

VARIATIONS ON A PARAPHRASE

Beauty foreign, my heart
empty. Love signaling
from her face.

In a grassy clearing, the woods
crying *Waste. Why
bother?*

In the shade of a beech, I
come to myself,
empty, turn back. It
is almost noon.

. . .

And while in this wise I
meditate, the tables are laid, nigh
on to noon. She holds my
head between her hands, as if
thunderstruck.

.

As for the front steps, they must always
be an odd number, so that the right
foot—with which one mounts
the first step—will be first to
reach the temple.

.

Beauty cries out, crying
with a foreign accent. Before
the head, within the body, with-
out pitch.

Between fall and rise, without
pitch. Consider well
the enormity of
what we must brook.

.

Bold knights, who've not their
hearts in their boots, and a thousand
foot, in a grassy clearing, foot-
loose. *Why?* Full
speed, says the king on the third
day of battle. Unaccented
syllables, rapid, my
heart empty.

.

Building, so far from shore, these
shadows of the high sea waves.

.

The distress which these notes cause, the
central part swollen and un-
graceful, open to the sky,
without a roof. When tiles are
broken or thrown down by
wind, we may yet be
preserved intact.

The doors are latticework. Ex-
traordinary cadenzas, ornaments
serving to connect the notes,
enliven them, em-
phasize, elucidate. Without them the best
melody might appear meaningless and
empty.
.

A good retreat. Love
faces signals, would destroy
the gardens round the town. Tell
how great a madness: machines for
war, armor, salted
meat, a heap of the whole, the whole
set on fire, blasted,
dishonored, written down, greatly
dissatisfied. Now, faced with
noon, come awe-inspiring pronouncements in
love's unmistakable mispronunciation.
.

Heavenly houses should be
arranged so that passersby
can glimpse the gods.

If solid ground can
not be found, nothing but loose or
marshy earth to the bottom, then
it must be dug up, set with pilings
of charred alder, olive, oak. A dim
scale indeed, ascending hole
by hole, admitted only as passing notes.

.

If they touch, they
begin to rot.

.

Inky darkness discovered in
the doorway. In
such cases, love
signals: did you
see her yesterday? did you see
how pale she looked? does
she like dogs? have you
put the kettle on? My
heart in my boots.

.

In unison on the right, on
the left in counterpoint.

.

Low, broad, clumsy-roofed: let the
width of the front be
divided into eleven
parts and a half.

Many processions re-
joice the heart, conduct us
safely to the earth.
.

My harangue scarcely
pitched, I'm
troubled. No music from these
times remains. *Why
bother?* In spring
all the trees become
pregnant, lap up water, return
to their natural strength.
.

One must not build temples
to the same rules to
all gods alike. While
Valentine Snow plays, we
dispense with space, with absolute
pitch, with a steady scale.
.

On the lowest tier, up the
curving slope, at the top of the hill,
right in the center, there is
a mistaken idea,
colossal, out of
place, of remarkable clarity.

Players behave differently. But
still the temple is
empty with an emptiness
like the sun at noon. Exactly the
pitch of my own voice. Void, I
marvel in this marvelous
waste.

.

Rise or fall.

.

Speed, says the shade. Such
syllables within the body.

.

Spring infects us on the extreme
left, an evolution
of temperament.

.

Such delight in foreign
music—a taste for
exotic timbres. Between
the entire body and its separate
members, we have nothing but
respect, so vital
the delicate vacillations.

This arrangement involves
dangers: continuous
glide, columns cracked by
reason of the great
width of the intervals. Too
sensitive to permit any
answers, roaming across
Mitteleuropa, having no
rules for pain . . .

.

Toward noon, I turn
to this tremendous beech and
move into its shade.

.

We counteract ocular
deception by an adjustment
of proportions, the air seeming to
eat away and diminish the shaft.

.

We have no example of this.

.

What's there to
follow? Will you
come? At the sound of the
horn, perfect
peace restored.

With due regard to
diminution, let a line
be drawn. The higher the eye has
to climb, observing more anxious
values of symmetry, the less
easily can it make its way
through the thicker and
thicker mass of air, long
reiterations of single notes, con-
structed out of old roofing tiles.

. . .

Sun nearly to
noon, I turn
aside, seek shade.

Why follow
nothing? Why
waste the woods' green cry?

Love signals, but my heart
is empty, beauty
foreign.

PLUMMET

The City Walls

Easy river, as the age
breaks on its shore. To the
solid bottom. Towers project beyond
a line of wall, attaining
quiet.

Bind faces like
pins: square towers
shatter. Chimerical, over-
taxed, immersed in a
sea of uncertainty, happiest
kid in the world: doctrine
of fools.

As the blood, even so
the sea has a constant
pulse or agitation. Towns
should be circular—angles
protect enemies.

Now a second foundation: flint, rubble,
burnt or unburnt brick. The burden of
earth, distributed. A faultless wall
built to last forever, plunging
my arm into the bubbling
cauldron. O creature
of water. And this spermatic Ocean fills
all that space which we thoughtlessly
attribute to the Air.

The Directions of the Streets

Exclude wind
from the alleys. Cold
winds are disagreeable, hot winds
enervating, moist winds unhealthy.

Remarks on the Winds

A mild thick air, unwavering
steadiness—back and forth—constantly
blowing. Augmenting our
oars. Far more
merciful than hanging, pupil
of enamel upon a
ball of silver, love of the possible.

In the midst of
the city, at about the fifth
hour, seize
the shadow. Shorten
the years.

Describe a circle. Universal, therefore
imperfect. So
situated, perplexed, in the
highest excitement, un-
interrupted.

Lay your streets and alleys between
the quarters of two winds. Then
constant blasts from the open
country will sweep through in violence thus
broken and dispersed, air-
cushioned divan. Without definite
purpose. How
unsearchable the quest.

Perfectly nude. How
like Mrs. Jay.

More on the Winds

Laws against
seduction, beauty, affection,
gentleness. A kneeling angel holds
a shell. Those who know names for
many winds take here as
center. Early morning:
humid air climbing, confusing
curses to come. Those who float,
spirals or interlacing circles: the shell
holds water.

The Sites for Public Buildings

Tides of titles. If the city
is on the sea, choose
harbor, temples, emporium, structural
features on a diminutive
scale, angelic figures with out-
stretched wings, at the angles
of the bowl beneath its
lower rim. Fresh fragmentary
things, but there are
other ways.

Many ancient fonts, perishing.

To make the image, set
the image on its feet. The wave
smites with such force, rich in
recollected and forgotten agonies. The
gods at the circus
command a view.

That the worship of Venus might be
free from the terror of fire.

The Macedonian Architect

Dark forms of belief. I have
made a design: to shape Mount
Athos into the statue of a man.

In his left hand a city, in his right
a bowl for all the water of all the
streams from the whole mountain, so that it might
pour
from the bowl into
the sea.

Vitruvius

Tendency of the times. The undeveloped
man conceals his very existence. Oh
certainly, says Mrs. Jay. Eternal passive
soul alongside an
active but unconscious mind.

But as for me, I
suffer with others, wait
for the shadow to
lessen and grow again, equal
to its length. We appear again
in commentary.

The Origin of the House

Wild beasts in woods, caves, groves, live on
savage fare, terrified by trees rubbing their
branches one against another. Description
of evil: busy hum. Watchfulness
has stages: flight,
yes,
silence.

(Utterance of sound purely
individual, articulate words indicating
things in common.) In this chance way,
we begin to talk.

Following the clue back-
ward. A desperate exterior melody. In that
first assembly, not obliged
to walk with faces to the ground,
we point out to each other that
our roof will not withstand
the coming winter's rains.

Space for the Dwelling

Forked stakes connected by
twigs, covered with
mud. Walls of mud,
iron, brass, silver,
gold. To summon fire, wide
target of our bosoms.

Entire trees flat on the ground,
leaving between them
interstices, wantonly destroyed or degraded to
base uses. Engineer. En-
chanter. Others readily as
myself could reach their destination by
will. Rowing their skiffs.

We build high towers, rude
form of the tortoise, give up
huts and begin to build houses.

Of the Primordial Substance

Thales thought water. Heraclitus (the
Dark) thought it was fire. So
entirely do they sympathize, everything
loses its power to charm, transport.

Bodies that cannot be
harmed, cannot
be cut up. Throughout time e-
ternal they retain an infinite
solidity. Halfway toward no
other pathway. Un-
certainly on the walls.

Make no mistake.

Brick

Heavy, washed by the
rain, they go to pieces.

So vividly are pictured scenes from the life of
Christ as
if about to open marble lips.

There are bricks which float.

Sand

Crackles when rubbed in the hands. I
speak only of sand fresh from the
sandpits. Who dare predict
wild dreams for the
perfect contemplation of a sounding body?

There must be pauses.

Lime

All bodies are composed—tough from
moisture, from the fire brittle. He
could well say nothing, his prayer
the entire desert.

Glad I'm not an angel, strength
burnt out, set free, pores
open, exhausted. Empty. This
would not be so unless
the mountains had beneath them huge
fires of brimstone, suddenly.

In a circular temple, dome or
cope of stars, I saw a thick
mist, resembling
ages on earth, very unlike the
world we left. Ours.

So the fire mixes,
hardens,
bores, swells, over-
flows, vomits forth. In the
mountains, intense heat, not
to suit man's pleasure but by
chance distribution.

Pozzolana

Wonders, it would seem, only that
the mind is still
connected, interweaving oceans, ornaments.

The force of fire, passing through the
fissures in soft stone,
sets it afire. Soft and delicate
burns out. Hard
parts are left. Burning makes ashes, carbuncular
sand.

Both are excellent. Tell me, kind
friend, the story of your life.

Stone

It is an old story, how wide-
spread the havoc wrought. I have
spoken of lime, of sand, of
dimension. Stone and rubble come
next. I am astonished: a diaper
of Celtic design.

There are several
kinds, mere transient
forms, less perfect
actual, quotations, vague un-
regulated heart. I want to
sit and listen, sailing.

Some soft. Red and black. White which
can be cut with a toothed saw. Frost
and rime crumble them. On the
seacoast salt dissolves, devours.

When fire penetrates, expels
the air, occupies the
empty spaces, there comes a great
glow and the stone
burns as burn the particles
of the fire itself.

Lightly, for there's no substance, only
momentary apparition.

In walls, use rubble.

Methods of Building Walls

Smallest stones, puddled with
mortar made of lime and
sand, abundance of lime and sand. Lime
and sand separate, dis-
unite, and the wall
becomes a ruin.

Several Monuments

In the course of time, mortar
loses strength: so monuments
tumble down, go to pieces. Mid-
passage: indigo,
cotton, tobacco, flower
vases in gardens, pig troughs
in farmyards or other
secular purposes, all to the same
stream of thought.

Joints loosen. Mere
heaps of material.

Now we see other
suns, corpse
of the central star, felicity
not in the operations of art.

Need fuels old-fashioned communities where
quaint traditions cling
among men with-
out culture: life on Mars, the light
lurid, red as blood.

Walls of Beauty

Such walls cannot
last more than years.

Epilogue: Stone Angels

Swan Point Cemetery, Providence, Rhode Island

for Barton Levi St. Armand

Angels go—we
merely stray, image of
a wandering deity, searching for
wells or for work. They scale
rungs of air, ascending
and descending—we are a little
lower. The grass covers us.

But statues, here, they stand, simple as
horizon. Statements,
yes—but what they stand for
is long fallen.

Angels of memory: they point
to the death of time, not
themselves timeless, and without
recall. Their
strength is to stand
still, afterglow
of an old religion.

One can imagine them
sentient—that is to say, we may
attribute to stone-hardness, one after the
other, our own five senses, until it spring
to life and
breathe and sneeze and step
down among us.

But in fact, they are
the opposite of perception: we
bury our gaze in them. For all my
sympathy, I
suppose they see
nothing at all, eyeless to indicate
our calamity, breathless and graceful
above the ruins they inspire.

I could close my eyes now and
evade, maybe, the blind
fear that their wings hold.

The visible body expresses our
body as a whole, its
internal asymmetries, and also the broken
symmetry we wander through.

With practice I might
regard people and things—the field
around me—as blots: objects
for fantasy, shadowy but
legible. All these
words have other meanings. A little
written may be far too
much to read.

A while and a while and a while, after a
while make something like forever.

From ontological bric-a-brac, and
without knowing quite what they
mean, I select my
four ambassadors: my
double, my shadow, my shining
covering, my name.

The graven names are not their
names, but ours.

Expectation, endlessly
engraved, is a question
to beg. Blemishes on exposed
surfaces—perpetual
corrosion—enliven features
fastened to the stone.

Expecting nothing without
struggle, I come to expect nothing
but struggle.

The primal Adam, our
archetype—light at his back, heavy
substance below him—glanced
down into uncertain depths, fell in
love with and fell
into his own shadow.

Legend or history: footprints
of passing events. Lord,
how our information
increaseth.

I see only
a surface—complex enough, its
interruptions of
deep blue—suggesting that the earth
is hollow, stretched around
what must be *all the rest.*

My "world" is parsimonious—a few
elements which
combine, like tricks of light, to
sketch the barest outline. But my
void is lavish, breaking
its frame, tempting me always to
turn again, again, for each
glimpse suggests more and more in some
other, farther emptiness.

To reach empty space, think
away each object—without destroying
its position. Ghostly then, with
contents gone, the
vacuum will not, as you
might expect, collapse, but
hang there,
vacant, waiting an inrush of

reappointments seven times
worse than anything you know, seven other dimensions
curled into our three.

But time empties, on
occasion, more quickly than
that. Breathe in or out. No
motion moves.

Trees go down, random and
planted, the
way we think.

The sacrificial animal is
consumed by fire, ascends in greasy
smoke, an offering
to the sky. Earthly
refuse assaults
heaven, as we are contaminated by
notions of eternity. It is as if
a love letter—or everything I
have written—were to be
torn up and the pieces
scattered, in
order to reach the beloved.

No entrance after
sundown. Under how vast a
night, what we
call day.

What stands still is merely
extended—what
moves is in space.

Immobile figures, here, in a
race with death, gloom about their
heads like a dark nimbus.

Still, they do—while standing—
go: they've a motion
like the flow of water, like
ice, only slower. Our
time is a river, theirs
the glassy sea.

They drift, as
we do, in this garden so swank, so grandly
indiscriminate. Frail
wings, fingers too fragile. Their faces
freckle, weathering.

Pure spirit, saith the Angelic
Doctor. But not these
angels: pure visibility, hovering,
lifting horror into the day,
to cancel and preserve it.

The worst death, worse
than death, would be to die, leaving
nothing unfinished.

Somewhere in my life, there
must have been—buried now under
long accumulation—some extreme
joy which, never spoken, cannot
be brought to mind. How else, in this
unconscious city, could I have
such a sense of dwelling?

I would
raise . . . What's the opposite
of Ebenezer?

Night, with its crypt, its
cradlesong. Rage
for day's end: impatience,
like a boat in the evening. Toward
the horizon, as
down a sounding line. Barcarolle,
funeral march.

Nocturne at high noon.

Acknowledgments

Some of this work first appeared in *Aerial, Avec, Caliban, Central Park, Cold Water Business, Conjunctions, Furnitures, Hambone, Infolio, Lace Neck Review, New American Writing, O.blek, Seaweed Thrown against the Pier, Sink, Sulfur, Temblor,* and *Tyuonyi.*

Shipwreck in Haven was published by Awede in 1989.

Falling in Love through a Description was published in a French translation by Françoise de Laroque (Paris: Créaphis, 1995).

Stone Angels was published as a chapbook by Instress in 1997, with photographs by Edward Holgate.

ALSO BY KEITH WALDROP

A Windmill near Calvary (University of Michigan, 1968)
The Garden of Effort (Burning Deck, 1975)
Windfall Losses (Pourboire, 1977)
The Ruins of Providence (Copper Beech, 1983)
The Space of Half an Hour (Burning Deck, 1983)
A Ceremony Somewhere Else (Awede, 1984)
Hegel's Family (Station Hill, 1989)
Shipwreck in Haven (Awede, 1989)
The Opposite of Letting the Mind Wander (Lost Roads, 1990)
Light While There Is Light (Sun and Moon, 1993)
The Locality Principle (Avec, 1995)
Analogies of Escape (Burning Deck, 1997)
The Silhouette of the Bridge (Avec, 1997)
Haunt (Instance, 2000)
The House Seen from Nowhere (Litmus, 2000)
Semiramis If I Remember (Avec, 2001)
Songs from the Decline of the West (in *No* #1, 2003)
The Real Subject (Omnidawn, 2004)

WITH ROSMARIE WALDROP

Well Well Reality (Post-Apollo, 1998)
Ceci n'est pas Keith, ceci n'est pas Rosmarie (Burning Deck, 2002)

Reversal by Claude Royet-Journoud (Hellcoal, 1973)

The Notion of Obstacle by Claude Royet-Journoud (Awede, 1985)

If There Were Anywhere but Desert: Selected Poems of Edmond Jabès (Station Hill, 1988)

État by Anne-Marie Albiach (Awede, 1989)

Ralentir Travaux by André Breton, Paul Eluard, and René Char (Exact Change, 1990)

Boudica by Paol Keineg (Burning Deck, 1994)

Objects Contain the Infinite by Claude Royet-Journoud (Awede, 1995)

Click-Rose by Dominique Fourcade (Sun and Moon, 1996)

Elegies by Jean Grosjean (Paradigm Press, 1996)

Sarx by Pascal Quignard (Burning Deck, 1997)

(with Wang Ping et al.) *Heart into Soil* by Xue Di (Burning Deck and Lost Roads, 1998)

Prose Poems [1915] by Pierre Reverdy (In *Untitled* #2, 2001)

Mental Ground by Esther Tellermann (Burning Deck, 2002)

(with Wang Ping et al.) *An Ordinary Day* by Xue Di (Alice James, 2002)

(with Wang Ping et al.) *Another Kind of Tenderness* by Xue Di (Litmus, 2004)

An Earth of Time by Jean Grosjean (Burning Deck, 2006)

Figured Image by Anne-Marie Albiach (Post-Apollo Press, 2006)

The Flowers of Evil by Charles Baudelaire (Wesleyan University Press, 2006)

(with Rosmarie Waldrop) *The Form of a City Changes Faster, Alas, Than the Human Heart* by Jacques Roubaud (Dalkey Archive, 2006)

Theory of Prepositions by Claude Royet-Journoud (La Presse, 2006)

(with Waverly, Wang Ping, et al.) *Zone* by Xue Di (Yefief World Edition, 2006)

Paris Spleen: Little Poems in Prose by Charles Baudelaire (Wesleyan University Press, 2009)

designer Lia Tjandra
text and display Adobe Garamond
compositor BookMatters, Berkeley
printer and binder Maple-Vail Book Manufacturing Group